Alicia Zukofsky

THE GREAT PISSER
& OTHER POEMS

STONYBROOK EDITIONS

Alicia Zukoksky, The Great Pisser and Other Poems.
Selected and edited by Karen Wittstock.

Herstellung und Verlag:
BoD – Books on Demand, Norderstedt
ISBN: 978-3-7347-2816-7

Nous devons surmonter notre rage et dégoût,
nous devons les faire partager, afin d'élever et d'élarger
notre action comme notre morale.

- René Char

FIN DE SIÈCLE

Trecking through
            deep ravines
then, places
    where a glacier left its
                    rocky trace
of fossils, deep sea animal
        creatures, of shallow bays
            breaking, creaking under rubber soles
caoutchouc, from rain forests
        processed in Northern plants
        by huge machines, you know
                never, by human hands

    Confused thoughts flashed up
    a voice shouting, no singing
        at the back of the mind
        of *blood,* on a far-off track

When, at the close of the century,
                you approach Grosny
        the stench of urinals
    the heritage of an
        all-too-German war carried
                into foreign lands
        envelops the torn, bruised'

            burned fragments of
        a stray dog in the street

Invisible, voices
        calling from somewhere
    Calling, it seems
        for an end
            to this suffering

Jan. 13, 2000

ARRIVING, AT THE CLOSE OF A CENTURY

Selvas deforestadas, erosion carving
   tree house dreams out of
         Northern Californian ridges
where shadow plays are staged
      by *los Araucanos de la C.I.A.:*
   Cocain rangers, full of
visions of ice-cooled
            Coca Cola fluid
         bottled in distant lands
         transported
         by planes, pack mules
            through the Mexican desert

In the shadow of shacks
   signs, blinking *Last exit, Nogales*
I saw you again, *gringo*
      counting greenbacks
         your official bonuses
No bigger drug-dealer, today
      than the State
      selling its omnipotence
            to sleazy policemen

Open your eyes, you buggers
What are you getting these days but
      a *bartered* society?

   Sold out, they say, are decency
& the common sense of communities

while the word "community" has become
a prescription drug
for the rich
those who are cowering now
behind the barbed wire
of their *Angst*

Jan. 14, 2000

IN THE STREETS OF BISHKEK

1

the icy blue
    gave way to spring clouds
the mountain snow
      brilliant as ever
           in the sun

But programmed ideas,
of beauty, fortune, individual progress
    crowd the minds
of the girls coming down
         the sidewalk

Perhaps, today
shoes with soles thicker than a brick
signify the new heights attained by humanity
    signify the
common denominator,
        of a *world culture*

2

Socialism? How foolish
can you be, to
believe, in the old
    discredited ideas?

But in Germany,
        in a county hospital
    the old, homesick Kirgiz -
blacksmith, *in the fifth generation* -
remembers how electricity came
            to his kolchoz, during the
                Brezhnev era

The Brezhnev years were good, he says
A bus driver in Frunse earned
    280 rubels per month
and the rubel was worth
            3 Deutsch Marks

    Perhaps this is not exactly
    a sound concept of Socialism
But it came close, for him
    to decent, improved
                living standards
    in a society that had been
    paternalistic or autocratic
    long before Brezhnev's time

                Jan. 13, 2000

THE GREAT PISSER

*a poem in remembrance of the release from
custody, by a foreign secretary, Cook, of a mass-
murderer, because of his incontinence*

an old man,
                    in his eighties
          held together by his uniform
held together, by his belief in
          Milton Friedman's medicine and
                    military virtue

          awaiting extradition in London
the slaughterer sits cozily on a couch
          pissing into the cushions
                    wetting his pants
          afraid as a chicken to be sent to Spain
          to be asked to stand up
                    and face
                              at last,
          his responsibilities
                    his shame
          his betrayal of a
                    President duly elected
                              by the people

          The *soldateska* of a century is
                    symbolized by an old man
          the "progress of humanity"

standing to attention, always at the disposal
of stiff upper-lipped dwarfs with a baton
    in their bloody hands.

    Here we get, finally
          the idea of a great
    millenium show, a tattoo for liberty
  Friedman's liberty, which is to say *that of the*
  market, and the human rights of
    truck-owning people
who created disorder in poor Chile
  toppling its hopes, toppling its
    attempt to finally free itself
of the big *supermercado* power in the North
  where Kissinger was pulling the strings
    where Reagan was looking down south
        hoping to see
  that America's colony was put in order
    The house of the *Gestapo*
  the house of ss-like *dignidad*
  where they're now digging for skulls
Westinghouse was glad to provide the
  instruments for electrical torture
glad to magnify the cries of the victims
    whose heads,
        shoved down
              the toilet
    smeared,
      with shit
were pulled up, alive or suffocated
    to ask the question,

DO YOU CONFESS?
DO YOU CONFESS?
DO YOU CONFESS?

The 20th century drawing to a close
  the times of the inquisition superimposed on
   the horrors of Oranienburg's KZ
  the horrors of Auschwitz and Oradour
Yes, the new advisors trained you well
  in the School of the Americas
  The silence of
    Georgia's sharecroppers
     in the face of continued racism
  mingles with the silence of *socker stadiums*
Five feet below the watered lawn of
  cloudy Santiago de Chile
  the vanished victims of Pinochet are rotting
  messengers for the 21st Century
   heralding the sweetsecret
  that the plain man is still nailed to the cross
   if he dares to join hands with his fellow man
    nailing his note of protest
    to the door of the mighty

  I LOOK BACK TO YOU
  20TH CENTURY
and I find you are best described
  as the century of the great pisser
  an old, stubborn man
   at the service of Kennicott Copper
   and similar concerns

Ready to kill the innocent
    Ready to confuse right and wrong
    Ready to break his oath of loyalty
    Sworn to a democratically elected president
        he had promised to defend
Ready to sell his country to the highest bidder
    in this age of unleashed "globalization"
        which is just another word for
        a world market developing
        crazily, chaotically, in ever new
    steps and stages since the 17th century
when Europe's galleons sailed east
        and south and west

    The big pisser,
        there in his London hospital -
    the frail symbol of servile power
    symbol of so many Prodis
        Schröders, Thatchers, and Mitterrands
    generals, directors on the boards of
            big corporations
    the big pisser is the one who
    even in defeat remains triumphant
Keeping the secret
        of his American bosses
as Lyndon Johnson kept the secret of whooo
    killed Kennedy and why.
The family of Martin Luther King
    knows better than you and I.
And the files opened now to the public
on U.S. involvement in the Allende assassination

tell only a fraction of the truth.
But so much is clear:
They learned their lesson well from the
Nazi murderers they let escape
to Canada and the U.S.
They learned their lesson well
from the Japanese specialists
of unit eight three three.
Experiments with live human bodies
have provided
valuable knowledge
to the powerful of today.

It is not innocently
they remained in control for so long
singing sweetly of democracy
singing sweetly their mermaid song
of luxury and marketed dreams.

Somewhere in the Argentine Alps
a near-sighted Kissinger dines with Turner
and the kids of Old Fonda.
Raising a toast, grinning broadly
leaning back in the pleasant late afternoon air
Here's to you, ye old pisser, they shout
And here's to Jack Straw, our buddy
that clever fox in
mist-filled, nebulous London!
From the kitchen, amazed faces
stare at the strange gringos on the veranda:

"Here's to you, old pisser? What do they mean?"
   The elites are bound, you see,
            by a common code of honor
      just as formerly, in the 18th century
      members of secret societies
            were affiliated
         by way of their oath.

Jan.13, 2000

AS A CENTURY DIES

The times -
not the London Times
not the New York Times either
the times, merely
no paper
no linear process
no circular
no circular process
the times, the times
ah, the times, do you
remember now
the days of old
so bitter then
so sweet and good
so good and old?

But my old man was 4 years old
when World War One started
with headlines and a
big bang
and inane shouts of
brain-deficient youngsters
& grandmother ran
to the victory celebration
at the Bismarck Tower in Herford
in September nineteen fourteen
only to be ashamed later
while grandpa was a young recruit
sick to death

by his own, self-concocted medicine
that would save him from the war
a young man
  with a clear mind
  a pacifist
    a socialist
  a participant, later
in the big carpenters' strike
  who'd die so early
  when he ran his motorcycle
    a few years later
  against the rear end of
a fog-hidden truck parked
  at the roadside
  in the middle of the
    dreary night

*   *   *

In the night's fog
Paul arrived
        was it in '41?
in what they called
    Mauthausen in that age of darkness
        that age of the plague
        a plague spreading
            from the hearts of people
        affecting their minds
            affecting their deeds

It made Paul

a Communist in '45
somebody who welcomed
the liberation of his country
by the Red Army

How soon
he would open his eyes!
How soon
they would open his eyes!

When Slansky died
and others with him
and the course of history
reverted to a position
where the *same* appears
to reappear again

the *same* cruelty
the *same* inanity
the *same* oppression

only *this* time
we are standing on our heads

only *this* time
everything is reflected in
a glistening mirror
brown turns to red
as the wound opens
and the oppressors are dangling
from their gallows

red turns to brown
as the wound closes and
the old poisonous drives
  pulsate in the body
the *jailer*, in us
  conversing
with our *jailed past*

*   *   *

It will all come back, dad sd
  as he talked to Siegfried
the survivor
  the *'half-jew'*
    as the killers had called him
the man who wanted
            (free now, he thought)
  to raise his children
    in the *Mosaic faith*

It *did* come back
Hate of strangers
Rejection / of The Other
It did come back
But now
as you read this
  the others are
  Albanians arriving in Bari
    Gypsies from Czech towns
      on their way to London
    Africans burned alive in Lübeck

The past has not died
IT IS ALIVE, IN US
IS WILL SURVIVE US, EVEN
a poisonous virus
passed on by humanity
as it proceeds -
progresses -
into the 21st century

Jan. 14, 2000

LIKE WILD GEESE

like wild geese
    darting South
  at the end of autumn
we saw planes sprint
    through the sky colored by
   a glowing sunset
  spreading reds and pinks
    and shades of orange into
   a translucent blue

where are they all headed, these planes -
  drawing their silvery streaks into the blue?

Well, you say
   with a yawn
 each one is headed
    to its destination
   following its charted course
    bound by a
        timetable
    in a calculated & reasonable way

Each one, carrying so many individuals
   called *passengers*
  is offering a bridge
    between a point of departure
    and a point of arrival
  is replacing what was once
  a *pilgrimage*, a *journey*

perhaps even
a *passage* involving
its own rites

Today, *rites of passage*
from one stage of *experience* in life
to the next
from one *innocence*
to its loss
from mourning to laughter and
if you can & will,
back again
seem to take place in airport lounges
as you sift through your hand baggage
wondering what you forgot
or what superfluous item
you chose to pack

The wild geese, on their way in the endless sky
are carrying their vital feathers
the minimum of food required for the trip
in their stomachs
no superfluous ounce
of extra fat
as they approach southerly coasts
dreaming of stays in a
far-away, yearned-for
habitat

Jan. 14, 2000

THE PAST IS PRESENT, STILL

which is why
the girl spoke of *Cheju dao*
Cheju
the island in the blue
the Paradise
where old women
keep the secrets
of *shamans*
where they keep
the memory of
past things
longer
than elsewhere
as they dive into the sea
as they harvest its riches
crabs and what-not
algae
used as a *coat*
for rice balls

The stories told
are told like rice balls
coated by algae
You see the black side of history -
Underneath
you taste
its white and sweet beauty

You listen

to the black side of history
Underneath
you remember
its white and sweet beauty

In the night, the old ones told
the truth about the days
when more than 60,000 islanders
were slaughtered by Syngman Rhee's killers
and the U.S. advisers stood by
In the night
they told the story
of more than one hundred
elected officials of their island
killed by firing squad
in Taejon's prisons
The island's self-rule smashed

But the tale of the dark days
of July, nineteen fifty
like a cocoon
hides and preserves
the half-forgotten truth
that the great commonwealth of the people
was flourishing
during the brief days
when liberty
was real

14/1/2000

TONIGHT, THE STORM

Tonight, the storm
   toppled the fir tree
  in the backyard
It broke, splintering
  with a hissing, creaky noise
  The wind clapped spoon-like
   on the big table
     of the unruly roof
Clattering, tiles answered
    with a deep and
     resounding song
    drumming their nervousness
      into the night

In Southerly France, the paper said
   the next morning
  pylons were felled
    of large overland lines
   cutting off electricity
     for tens of thousands

But for all the suffering
  brought by this
unprecedented outburst of nature
  the *economy, strangely enough,*
  is so much better off
   for its own reasons

Nature may run amuck

as more and more carbon dioxide emissions
reach higher strata
of the atmosphere

but the repairs thus occasioned
swell the coffers
of clever
entrepreneurs

Jan. 1, 2000

ANGOLAN ELEGY

the riches of a country, oil, diamonds
feeding a war -
I see madness drilling huge
wounds into the land
see the earth sifted with the help of chemicals
poisoning rivers
I see *"elites"* smoking Dominican cigars
riding their shiny cars
from mansion to office and back

a war economy *under way*
a war economy of rebel and
government camp
engulfed in what today they call
"globalization"
*the vast, poisonous network
of international economic relations*
the *power* of money, the *greed* of
multinational corporations -
is this what *drives* it?

is it the speculation of shareholders
some of them people with
millions and millions of dollars
in their accounts
men & women
who don't pay taxes
if they find a way?

But Angola falls to pieces
        ripped apart
by the leopard and the 'gator
eaten up by the *"appetite for energy"*
        of the *First World*

There was a time
  there was a time, I learn
when young black intellectuals
    attending the universities of the East, of the West
  spoke earnestly of justice
the wonderful *grass roots movement*
            of the Angolan rebels
  with their make-shift schools, in the bush
    where they applied, creatively,
      Paolo Freire's method
  to make knowledge accessible, to *everyone.*
    To let everyone
          acquire dignity
              not *money.*
      To let the desire for freedom bloom!

  Where is it now –
that seriousness, that dream?
      Where is it now?
          Where is it?
      Where? o where?

          Jan. 15, 2000

NOT THE FIRST TIME

as the perspective grows dimmer
   for everything vital in this world
water
        clean air
   decent, affordable housing
an opportunity, for everyone
     to contribute, constructively
to the well-being
      of his community…

the share indexes
     rise to new heights
   in London Paris New York
not to speak of the recently founded
    towers of speculation
     for instance, in "red"
         Shanghai

   it is not the first time
that this kind of *exuberance*
   preceded *deep* and *destructive crises*
    it is not the first time
   in the 20th century -
and the 21st, it seems
     will provide no exception
     to the rule

    But the rule
      of course

of money-driven power –
of *capital*
            controlling *corporations*
and thereby, *lives* –

that rule is far from ended
as they continue
to build networks, linking
Davos, New York
and Bilderberg and Aspen
Rome, Gütersloh, and Tokyo

The greedy of the world are clever enough
to understand
the tools of disinformation
they have built their empires
                of *info-tainment*
clever pupils of Goebbels
clever pupils of the
                emperors of Rome
who knew why they provided
panem et circenses
to the hungry, cheated crowds

Jan. 14, 2000

AS A *WHIRLWIND CENTURY* CASCADES
INTO THE NEXT

"The important decisions are reached
by a few dozen, if not a handful of
men,
in a back-room"

Economic booms
        followed by economic crises -
T V news advertising
        the myopic outbursts of
                        "opportunity"…
the shadowy ghost of deluded *euphoria*
        circling above
                a cultural desert -

        At the end of a century
                propelled from war to war -
        colonial genocide to
                vast European genocide -

ten-thousandfold, slaughters in Nanjing,
        Vietnam, Iraq…

a man,
        renowned poet,
        cultured contemporary
        of the out-going *ancien régime*,
has said

We *should be riding the tide*
Up to it, he maintained
The achievements of the century
    mastered, well-comprehended.

Today
"the best men of our time"
are riding a tiger
that is uncontrolled, jumpy, dangerous
darting ahead -
    Not just the Dow Jones
during the longest boom in
    recent American economic history
    But worldwide temperatures -
        Drastic changes in the world climate -
        The growth of mega-cities -
        Their social and environmental
        problems -

Experts faced with
    what they call the
        population explosion
seem puzzled
    in Sub-Saharan Africa
    at the rate *Aids* is spread -
at the disappearance of
        entire generations -
Where they puzzled, as well
    when secret projects turned Katanga
    in the '70s
        into a test range

for cruise missiles?
What *else* did these military experts
of the U.S. test?
The *latest hypothesis* of how to stop
BLACK GROWTH
BLACK FERTILITY
in a world *dominated by*
WHITES?

Is it the old
racism
the old
fascist
superiority complex
that set free
a new round of genocide
a new scientific experiment
in the tracks of
Mengele
and his Japanese
imperial colleagues?

The times give us hard choices to make
We've grown wary of
conspirational theories
Today, the mighty of the world
know how to handle
the conspiracies of
nationalist or religious fanatics,
failing in their Afghan camps.

Today, the mighty and powerful
            have no need to conspire
What they engage in is
            concerted action
        bringing together
            the influential politicians
            and businessmen of the world
    In DAVOS for instance -
        In ASPEN
        In the Bernhardian Club
            at the Bilderberg Hotel
        where they reach decisions
            or effect what they call
            an exchange-of-ideas

    a step, once again
            towards asserting the hegemony
                of U.S. power

    Of course, it is a power
            divided by clashes of
                interest, at home
    Of course, it is a power
            forced to
        mediate when faced with
            a diversity of interests
                among allies

        It is the same, old
            diplomatic game
        Metternich tried to play

back in eighteen fifteen
Kissinger said so
He's a clever fox
A stupid, clever fox
And one of the many instrumental people
with *brains* (they say)
who are at the service of *BIG MONEY*

But *BIG MONEY*
in its *greed*
destroys us
destroys the *oikos* of humanity
EARTH
destroys the conviviality
the spirit of community needed
to make *EARTH*
habitable

So the century ends
worse than it began
Technological progress continuing
CAPITAL VASTER THAN EVER
MIGHTIER THAN EVER
MORE CONCENTRATED THAN EVER
AND MORE THREATENED

while the masses look forward
towards an uncertain future
haunted by illnesses
'natural' catastrophes
insecurity in their lives

groping attempts to orientate
themselves in a world
where they are, more than ever
kicked around -
the *objects* of history

whose course no one
not even the masterminds
in networked
and competing think-tanks
at the service of
international capital
can claim to control

Humanity, *the*
educated thinkers
at the end of another -
the 18th century
had dreamed,
would become conscious
of itself
its fate
Take it in its hands
rationally and
in the spirit of
égalité fraternité
They knew
liberté could not
exist
without the other two
Today

not only *liberty* --
survival
may not be possible
without them

But in their greed
in their blind clinging to
money, to power
the people put in charge
in Washington Rome
Tokyo Moscow Beijing
are steering the boat -
another *Erika*
in ill shape -
against the cliffs
of its Normandy

We'll have to wait and see
what the oil-spill will bring
An awakening or -
the ushering in of
more suffering more needless
avoidable
death

Jan. 19, 2000

FACING THE CYCLES

Revolutions
　　　ushered in the century
Nineteen-ten - Mexico
Nineteen-eleven - China
Nineteen-seventeen - Russia
　　　Nineteen-eighteen - Germany

Did they unleash
　　　a wind of change?
accelerate progress?
　or was it just that they brought
periods of brief or protracted
　　　counter-revolution?
　　　　　degradation?
　　　complications of
　　　　　　　history?
　　　　　drawn-out
　　　　　　　suffering?

If, as the image of the
　　　WHEEL
　　tells us
　suffering
　　　　gives birth to
　　　suffering only
　the wind of change
　　　felt, in those years
　still gave rise
　　　　to hopes

A feeling we cd make it
            NEW, perhaps
      more humane

            we
                  the species
      we, men & women
                  involved in the
                        shaping of
                  our own fate,
                              history

      Today
the hope seems to
                  evaporate
      fixed to the brief
                  and shaky attempts
      to make money
                  at the stock exchange

while others, mutely, toil
      in the office next door
                  or -
      connected by internet -
            in far-away
      Third World sweat shops

                        Jan. 19, 2000

THE APEX

Decisions reached
in backrooms
Conflicts coordinated -
Social-Democracy
co-opted
first in Japan, in nineteen-forty-five
and in Germany
then Latin America
and elsewhere

But the economy as
unharnessed as ever

the biosphere
the Great, Underlying
Material Mattress
of all our tiny actions
in history
convulsively gasps
reacts
to the combined
millionfold stupidity
of the human race

while CLEVER CLERKS
speak of
the End of History
the final triumph
of their

unscrupulous efforts
to sell intellectual prowess
to the highest bidder

The boat fights unruly seas
the captain's giving
assuring commands
as is the custom
in times of distress

Jan. 19, 2000

AGAIN, SHALLOW DESIRES

shallow desires
mistaken for dreams
centering around merchandise
The commodification of
the world
«You should consider yourself
as a product», they tell us
«Ask yourself
who needs you»
«Advertise yourself»

So here I tell you
who needs you:
It is, for instance
the man at ALCATEL in Stadthagen
whom they are going to sack
with thousands like him
creating distress
in an entire city

It is thousands and thousands of
people stricken by
"restructuring" ordered by the
I. M. F. in South Korea

It is: the poor of Surabaya -
hit by exploding food prices
and unattainable
cooking oil, priced out of reach

of the many

The technologies of tomorrow
announce more overproduction
ahead of the purchasing power of
the world's underpaid masses

The same mistakes repeat themselves
in the «global factory», as they
call it
as were witnessed
in the *Great Depression*
of the eighteen seventies
the crisis of nineteen hundred
or nineteen eleven

But the laws of exploitation *remain*
the propensity to protect property
remains
the elites or they who call themselves
elites
govern in the name of Capital -
Always the same clerks
killers if necessary
who command the assassination
of an elected President
who make nuns fly in the air
who snatch children from their
young mothers
raped and killed
by uniformed servants

The world has not changed, in that respect
since Herodes ruled
since Nero made his capital
a torch
to light the fire
of fear
in the hearts of his
subjects

In the 21st century
the media are prepared again
to light this fire
to steer the ship away
from the coasts of
Enlightenment

Jan. 19, 2000

MAYAN WISDOM

Mayan wisdom
at long last
is to revert to the community
to let it *regain life*

the flame *rekindled*
of compassion, of
sacrifice if necessary

not the heart, ripped out
for the fictitious gods
at the behest of governing priests
priests, close
to the governing

but the heart opened
to the complaints and sorrows
of a neighbor

his weighty burden
shared

Mayan wisdom, in the Lacandonian forest
is to overcome
strife in the community
individual efforts, to strike it rich
or share a little bit of
local power

with the powerful
as a headman
a burgomaster

Mayan wisdom
in this year of full moons
half moons
vanished moons and
silences

in this year of sunsets sunrises
rains tempests quakes
and eruptions, of volcanoes

in this year of elections
and stock market gains

Mayan wisdom is to return
to the tables of community
the tables of community
where the crucified people
is, finally, being
reborn

Jan. 19, 2000

PEOPLE MEET IN BACKROOMS

while birds are chirping
in the early morning
even before sunrise
while birds are singing
expecting spring
People with energy and determination
meet in backrooms
deciding the fates of the country
People meet in backrooms
thinking they decide
the fate of the *earth*

But, as ever, politics is only a game
for people with hungry egos
thinking their will is decisive

Politics is only a game
for a few
convinced of their terrible
importance

And it is true
they *can* unleash wars
they *can* unleash interest hikes
they *can* open and close
frontiers to refugees
even though *gaps* remain

their action affects

the profit of the few
who try to keep
in close connection
with the centers
of political power

their action affects
the *way*
you & I
can gain our livelihood

Still, what they create
is a muddle
And for all their clarity
of decisions reached
their simplicity
of recipes propagated
the world, even that
of the *economy*
proves so much more
complicated and confused
as millions of actions entwine
as millions of chords are struck
producing
effects and counter-effects
in a chaotic
unforeseeable
again and again disruptive manner

So, against all intrigues of rich egotists
& all powerful attempts to

institute central planning
from above
what way out can there be
but *friendliness*
to increase friendliness in the world -
cooperation
to increase well-being
in the world -
togetherness
to ward off
difficulties & dangers
commonly faced ?

In a world divided
into rich and poor -
hungry and overfed people -
FRIGHTENED
& FRIGHTENING FORCES
will continue
to wreck havoc

In a world where the powerful
are concerned to maintain their power
and the rich
to maintain their riches
all will lose,
in the end -
everything

Jan. 19, 2000

AT THE END

At the end of the 20th century
democracy has been bought
It is not possible anymore
to become President of
the richest & freest land of the world
if you shun Whitewater deals
if you shun connections that help yr wife
to make, say, 3 million dollars out of
ninety thousand,
in a year
Which is to say, you have to have *friends*
or be a multi-millionaire yourself
to run for office
with a goddam fuckin' chance
of success

Everyone knows it now
And those who are tired of it
stay away from the polls

while those *with interests to protect*
and *stakes in the* res publica
throw their weight
behind *him*
who promises *the most*

And in Europe
the party machines
covet the help

of big business
Banks, trade &
industrial corporations
channel *untaxed money*
to politicians in power
and get their voices heard
their extra opportunities
to make additional profits
Undeterred by leaks and scandals
this game proceeds already
for decades
if not longer

and we all know Mercedes-Benz Corporation
steels industrialists, and the banks
backed Hitler's little group
until it was strong enough
to take over,
and prepare the big war

A wonderful opportunity for
Capital to deal with its crisis
of '29

Jan. 19, 2000

A TRIBUTE TO ROBERT KRAMER

exiled, in your own land
the wide expanses of the north, the west
I see you tracing
the long band of *Route One*
from small town to small town
broken asphalt, potholes -
broken promises

In Clarksville Mississippi
encountered the sales girl
in the super-mart
selling tapes
containing the canned
voices of
Blues musicians

She recounted her tale
of injury, in a land
free only *by name*

In Chicago
the Thai taxi driver
told his bitter tale
while we passed the lakeshore
on our way north

There was a time when...
Yes, there was a time when
Woody Guthrie would sing of

electrification

and the hopes attached
to the big new dams
in the Far West

There was a time when TVA
stood for dreams and promises
of a *better life*
not for the few
but everyone
who'd care
to tackle his job

In the '60s, the fight for
civil rights disproved them
The killing
of Martin Luther King
disproved them
The way the
Kennedy murder was
never clarified
disproved them
The war in Vietnam
disproved them

In the '70s, with Nixon ruling the country
the best minds of the land
left

and I remember Steven, in Athens, Greece

dreaming he cd forget the country
his father attained when he fled
NAZI Europe

Jan. 19, 2000

A BRIEF ACCOUNT AT THE FIN DE SIÈCLE

deals were done in that way -
a Pope
having his Cardinals channel
American money
to a Polish trade union
It broke the yoke of
military rule
merely to introduce another yoke -
that of NATO demanding
an increase in military expenditures
planes to be ordered
in the U.S.A.
while living standards
for most citizens
went down, in Poland

This is why Brent Scowcroft is again
in Gdansk
at the behest of the N.S.A.
and of some Republican big-shots
figuring in some committee called
International Republican Institute

Meanwhile, in Spain
the Ebert Foundation gave money
of similar if not identical origin
to Gonzales (trained in Germany)
and his P.S.O.E.
It guaranteed a smooth transition

after Franco's death
No chance
of people rising up
to demand *self-rule*
Not in the villages of
Andalucia
Not in the mining communities
of *Rio Tinto Corporation*

The 'Socialists,' with their methods of graft
and state-ordered murders
would be in charge of affairs
controlling *a span* of Spanish history

Today, they look to Bonn
wondering how much they have in common
with the C.D.U.
Or with those involved in the
Agusta affair, in Belgium
where killers of children
& businessmen dealing in
pictures of harassed and
tortured meat
brought to light how
deeply entwined they were:
those who attempt to make
money at any price -
and *the police -*
governors -
deputies
of political parties

- 58 -

All the while, in Italy
the old fox
accused of collaboration with the *mafia*
after he broke the *Gladio* news to the press
faced a witness released by the U.S. government
to do him in
They did not need him anymore
the old co-*combattante*
since they co-opted the P.C.I. bosses
during those sessions where Berlinguer
giving his talks in New York
at the Council of Foreign Affairs
proved *trustworthy*
to the *dominant "elites"* -

the *grave robbers*
of a fucked-up world

20/1/2000

A NEW AGE IS USHERED IN

All through the snowy night
         messages buzzed in the air
«Perch will arrive tonite»
         «He's practically stranded»
«We have him on our hook»
«He's gasping already
         Stranded on the beach
         Without a chance
              to reach again
                   open waters»

«He's finished»

The lake, mirroring the mountain
         lay peacefully next morning
foreshadowing the end of the century
                   the end of an era
Boxes filled with military hardware
         arrived safely on pack mules
         Carried down Alpine trails
              treasure troves
              reached safely
                   their destinations
The parties concerned
         were jubilant
dreaming of never-ending fêtes
         In his castle, the
         Chancellor of the empire
                        of dust

wore his smile like
an iron mask
when they asked him for the
whereabouts of his paladin
Stolenmountain, the brash friend
hiding, in the shadow
Shitfarmer, the head of the secret police
beaming innocently
in his backroom
when the secretary of the press
was breaking the news
to the press corps
selected members of the profession, that is
who'd report carefully
of the unfortunate accident

In the Alpine colony
A curate, inexperienced and young
would look into the unavoidable matter
Meanwhile
business would go on as ever
Other deals to be done
Other men, to be used
Other sums, safely collected
Stashed away, as
treasure troves
in Lichtenstein

The years would pass
The same gang in power

all of the time
financing their way to the top
again and again by the same
hidden funds
They did not dream yet
they would have
a Y two K problem

The events accelerated
The ruler - exchanged
The account books -
carried away quickly
from the government offices

In these times
at the end of the period
polo games ushered in
the New Age
(An age, as old and bloody, as ever)

Heads were offered
For instance, that of a
former *grande*
A head of the tribe
they showed, in ugly triumph
to the masses
like a Cabbage Head
on a Pole

20/1/2000

BIRTHDAY POEM

for Ernesto Cardenal,
in Nicaragua

movements bloom and degenerate
leaders prove their courage, show sacrifice
then end up, all too often, seduced
by power, and luxury
even the people, awakened by excessive injustice
turns again, to apathy and sleep -
The *sleep,* we know, that gives *birth*
to the monsters, of old
But an old man
a poet, in earthquake-shaken
flood-devastated Nicaragua
in his 75th year already
proves sane
and as compassionate, as ever

Like you, Ernesto
again and again
we encounter those
who give us hope
who pass on
the light of love
the light *lighting*
our search of justice
from one generation
to the next

Like you, Ernesto, we know
the voice of poetry is weak
but stinging, ringing
through the clatter of noise
produced, day by day
by the media

produced, by what they call
entertainment
the loud *hype*
of those who want to
drown out
consciousness
want to drown out
loneliness
want, or wanted
to give us
kicks

It is the kicks
in the ass we get -
the beatings, suffered
beatings seen
as others suffer -

millions, hundreds
of millions -

which make us
wake up, again

which make us
listen
to the sound of poetry
in our soul
the voice of God speaking
you would say
the voice
in our stubborn hearts

those tender
awakening hearts

It is this which makes us fight again
not necessarily with words
but also, like David, with the rock lifted
as we try to defend the weak
against Goliath, once again

The time will come, Ernesto
when the people of Nicaragua
the people of all Latin America
when the people of the world
will be free

free to sing and dance
and work and write poetry
in a brotherly spirit
but also free, to fall again
prey to those who covet
personal power

free to begin the *rondo* of
slavery and liberation, again

In my dreams, I see the paintings
by the lake
I see the community where you lived
This, not the fighting, the blood spilled
the injustice done, even by those
who longed for justice -
This-, this, Ernesto-, points the way
projects a vision
of tomorrow

21/1/2000

BRUNO

in nineteen twenty-five, Bruno was fifteen
a street-wise big-city kid,
                    in Berlin's northern outskirts
        collecting scrap with his buddies
        learning to draw, in the attic
                of a tenement house
            where his father put
                    heads, made of gypsum
                        on boxes, piled up
                in a well-lighted corner

        in nineteen twenty-eight, learned
to paint, in art school
                    its evening class
attended the classes of Hermann Duncker
reading *DAS KAPITAL* at the MASCH
    Of all those beginning the course
only 3 finished it
                    he among them

        That year, awakened by the
                            anti-semitism
            the militarism
                that was in the air
                even in Berlin
        he joined the party of Rosa Luxemburg
            a vivid party
            a party of academics, too

who adhered to their strange
professional language
foreign to the panelbeater
or the railroad worker
(He knew he had to *translate.*)

In 1933, of all those *more than
one hundred people* in his 'cell'
in Reinickendorf
just one remained, with him
fighting nocturnally
by gluing posters to
the walls of houses
carrying a gun in his pocket
for self-defense

In 1945, having survived the war
he met Achim
in a street
in Northern Berlin
Achim, the teacher's son
the young, enthusiast fascist
who, ashamedly, crossed over
to the other side of the street
answering, *Well, you know why*
when Bruno shouted *What's on, Achim
Don't you know me, anymore?*
It was then that Bruno remarked
*Let's wait and see
what crap will be forthcoming
from our side (the red).*

A little later
having participated
in meetings in Karlshorst
having talked again
with Pieck, his old teacher
with Mielke, the neighborhood kid
he quit

never to be actively involved again
in *organized* politics

21/1/2000

A BOUGHT & CORRUPTED CLIQUE

a bought & corrupted clique
"Socialists" like Mr Craxi
who do in
    the rank-and-file
abandoning the *scala mobile*
or allowing a crook
    like Mr. B
to assemble an empire
of television stations
    papers, journals
that sway "public opinion"

they cashed in
    hundreds of millions
    dollars *not lire*, dear
and got away with it, scot-free

It's the tip of the iceberg -
the wonderful *network*
    of *politicians*
    running our
    "democratic" societies
that *capital* has built -
A TWO-PARTY SYSTEM, MOST OF THE TIME
where the big players win
    no matter which horse makes it
They have 'em both
    on their pay list
Kohl or

Schröder

Bush or

Clinton

who cares

The money involved
seriously spent
on the maintenance
of power

Whose power?
The people's?
The guy's
who's in charge -
running the government?
Come off it, man
What sense would it make
to spend that lavishly on him
if he does what he wants
what he thinks is right
for the country.

Of course, they're on the look-out
for candidates who really think
what's good for them
is good for the country.
And still it's
a bought circus -
a rigged game -
we all know it
deep down in our hearts

And those who are bought
are a bigoted, clever crowd
they know how to
involve the Gestapo
if a trace points
to their darker
private lives

Think of Dutroux
think of
the vanished children

Think of Mitterrand
ordering the bombing
of the *Rainbow Warrior*

Think of
Oklahoma City
where an office building
had to explode
to stop the growth of
right-wing militias -
create the aversion needed
by "mainstream politics"
in their media offensive
against a rebellion of
cheated
hard-working guys -
the poor, devastated, debt-ridden
farmers and working-men
of the Midwest

dumb enough
to fall prey again
to dirty "recipes" of old

Those in power
are as unscrupulous as ever
Those in power
maintain merely a democratic façade
They NEED your VOTE
every FOUR years
The rest of the time
they need clever
intellectual whores
to keep a rotten
egotistical
capitalist game
from going down
the drains

All that counts is maintaining profit
Ah they know it's a snowball effect they build on
Ah they know it's a cardboard house
If it crumbles
and falls apart
there will be yells
& a gnashing of teeth

there will be trembles
that shake the earth

23/1/2000

THOSE WHO LOOK TO THE STARS

Those who look up to the stars
 tend to become
    mere visionaries
knowing the general direction of the way
 They often stumble
   over the merest irregularities
     of the road

 while, obsessed with the notion
    of progress
 others try to get ahead
Accelerating the number of steps
    taken each minute
 they make haste
   blindly
   just glad they get
     anywhere
  rushing down the most obvious
  cul-de-sacs

 There are those, of course, who
  afraid to stumble into an abyss
  progress carefully
     groping
   through the night
 Searching for pathways
  Searching for hidden tracks
  or comfortable roads

And for all their searching
            they forget to look up
      to the celestial bodies
      losing orientation

The experienced wanderers
      the scouts
    the awake travelers
        of course, know
  it is necessary to
            determine your location
      clarify the goal
          look up to the stars at night
      the sun's location in the sky
              during daytime walks
          while never, never
                losing their "feel"
                    for the ground -
        their astute awareness
            vis-à-vis the surprising realities
                of life

                    Jan. 21, 2000

WHAT WE SEE TODAY

What we see today
is the expression
            of social forces
Big money that rules
        Clerks that are for sale
    whether they be named
        Kissinger
            Andreotti
        or Clinton

The "conspiracies," by the way -
    only get-togethers
        of concerned experts
            devising "solutions"
        that are part of
            larger
                conflicting efforts
        parts of controversial
                strategies
            to defend *class interests*
    not those of *you & me*

As common people
    we know that -
And because we're so many
    and not quite so dumb
                all of the time
we have to be taken
                into account

Every four years at least
they have to throw
                    crumbs at us

        slogans

            signs of "good-will"

    while they laugh their heads off
        silently
                behind closed doors
    while they
            scoff, at the "mob"
        while they think
                all we need
            is "panem
                    et circenses"

                    Jan. 23, 2000

SPEAKING OF CLASS

The workers, of course
    are around
        same / as ever

But the bourgeoisie -
    Dissipated. Dissolved.
Underpinned only
        by its shadow
           of old

    Today
Vast Capitals are *the dog*
      that wags its tail
    of fund managers
        boards of directors
    the whole crew
      of clever young men
     dreaming of fast cars
     large salaries
      and bonuses

  who'd sell their lives
    their health
      their happiness
    for the maintenance of
      "the system"

It "flourishes,"
      they may think

being "the best of all worlds"
as it goes through
                    booms & crises
wrecking the
        natural household
            of this very *world*

In their imagination
            hidden investors
        large & small
count the *zeros* behind
                numbers written in their
                        account books
    Meanwhile
        the riches of the earth
    are squandered
The time runs out
    The misery of millions -
        growing day by day

It's a "successful system," indeed
    that piles up problem upon problem
                    it can't solve

while wealth is concentrated
capital amassed
    much of it, fictitious,
            speculative
    bound to vanish
        in another
            vast crisis

We've seen the trial run
      in East Asia in ninety-seven
We'll get more of it-
      you just wait & see

Jan. 23, 2000

LEAVES BREATHE

Leaves breathe
Like animals have
      a soul

and when our little experts
    of chemical warfare come
they *blow out*
      life's light
in the eyes of the animals
and when the little soldiers
    of chemical reaction arrive
they *hurt* the leaves
and the leaves turn pale
    and wither, in anguish
And our little soldiers of
    chemical reaction are jubilant
and our little experts of
    chemical warfare cry 'Victory'
and my cat
with its intense glow
    of love in her eyes
looks at me
and asks me, voicelessly,
    Why
why do you
    condone it?

Jan. 23, 2000

LANCELOT STRIKES AGAIN

I can see Princess Karen
Diane Silkwood riding downtown
in her white hearse
The station manager in London
has the report ready
The people in Houston
know
when she'll arrive
at the conference
They clap their hands
As ever, Lancelot is ready
to strike
There is the big *camion*
There is the black horse
of Lancelot and his gang
They put in a faster gear
They *push* her hearse
against the concrete wall
The wall *collapses*
Behind it
an empty landscape
of children, mutilated -
Landmines explode
At a distance, the plant
with the *contaminated* workers

Jan. 31, 2000

A HAPPY MID-CENTURY

born in a basement -
the father, dragged away
into war
foreseen ten years ago, in twenty-eight
When it broke out,
still tried to resist
Then succumbed
just trying to survive
a penal battalion's decimation

When I was not yet one
in May, he returned
The male adults, in the neighborhood
were taken away
to prison camps
It made us popular, indeed

Later, I lay awake
in a bunk, at Belsen
heard his voice mingle
with other voices
trying to tell the tale
of how they survived

Feb. 3, 2000

WADING, IN BLOOD

Roughly forty-thousand killed
two-hundred thousand tortured
this is what *it did* -
the regime of *Habre*

propped up by the U.S.A. and France
when they tried to "stem the tide of terrorism,
emanating from Libya"

Today, the truth leaks out
Always the same truth -
in Turkey
in Guatemala
in Ecuador, Bolivia, Peru
Brazil...
in Argentine. Or in Chile...

They are wading in blood.
In the "defense of
liberty,"
they are wading in blood.

They drowned it out -
pointing to Stalin's crimes
drowned it out, of our consciousness -
our knowledge

Which liberty did they mean
when they did it?

Which liberty, which
if not the *unlimited freedom to exploit -*
of their banks, their

corporations?

Feb. 9, 2000

DELUDED

In Knokke, I read in the papers
eight people - so long already
under the watchful
eyes of the State
"plotting", they say, to revive
an armed struggle of desperados

What kind of world are they thinking they face
in EURO-LAND?
A country ravaged for decades by
hunger, migrating peasants
robbed of their land
eager for a chance to
beg or work?
A land tortured by war lords
suffering under the onslaught of
invading armies?

Please ask
the taxi-driver
taking you from your hotel
to "hidden" bistro rooms
about his worries!

Please ask the unemployed
about the worries of their lives!

They care
for a functioning labor office

the punctual arrival of their checks
whatever their
justified complaints!

In a world ripped apart by conflicts,
plagued by injustice,
"EURO-LAND" is still
a "safe zone"
where workers go to work
and spend
and nag

Don't confound it, then
with the China of the Thirties
don't confound the mess
so many people find themselves in
with the sufferings of Africans
under Apartheid.

Things have to get a lot worse
before you'll get more
than the frustrations of
eight deluded people in Knokke
who can't imagine there are
other means *than arms*
to fight the
aspirations of *CAPITAL*
to intensify exploitation
& put us down, for good

20/2/2000

BIRTHDAY POEM

for Lena

these days of March
  Bremen
      jazz
the iron sound of
  a tram screeching
        to a halt

o what seemingly strange
  sight, offered today
  by the birds squawking
      in spring-time leaves

There goes that cloud again
  in front of your backyard windows
The kitchen sink is not
          running over
    The dreams of
  Michigan, Québec
are more real than the
  taxi hooting outside
      trying to take
    a memory away

            (March, 2000)

ONE OF THE YOUNG REBELS

The way I like it is
                    the way it is
says the inscription
                    on his bag

Yes, he *is* an *individualist*
    a *backpacker*
off to Nepal, perhaps, to
    Reno, to
            Disney Land

He knows, already
        everybody is special
& *we're all individualists*
        with those identical bags
        saying 4 YOU
        and ALL YOU NEED
        is what is on offer
        at the big stores
        Thank you, Capitalism
    Yes, Thank you, KAPUTALISM
    Thank you for all of it:
        You're Great

March 9, 2000

WITNESS

Certainly, a unique century.
He was terrified, nay-sayer deep down
Or perhaps a wanderer, in the realm of
Mythologies, of surprises, or perhaps
Saddening insights, as when
Karl Marx discovered **class relationships** as a key
Yes, that sort of thing, & To Continue, *undaunted*

April 17, 2000

TIME OF THE TOMAHAWKS

Kwangwoo told me
They stationed them in
Korea. When was that?

Time of the Tomahawks
of silv'ry chariots driving thru the sky
and yellow Chevrolets stopping in front of
the United Nations
where delegates in session vote
entranced by a slick careerist
and dozens more
in the aisles

This world-wide democratic farce
how is it, then
to achieve peace not
dreams shattered to pieces?

justice not the execution of the innocent
by marshals and justices of the peace
bought long ago
by the big ranchers
of a Western *cow town* nation
and their gangster-like offspring

Yes -
how is a poor little, opportunistic
career diplomat, from Africa
to ward off the pressures of the

Bushes, Reagans, or Clintons
with their ludicrous
schemes and grappling
for well-oiled power
and dollar-greased
domination?

April 17, 2000

HIGHLY SPECULATIVE

a century when
  philosophy withdrew
    into the glossy leaflets
      of corporations

whoever studied them closely
  knows we got a situation
    that is always improving
a *Metaphysics of Mores*
  written by the promoters of
    a *stock-exchange culture*

However, this much will be granted at long last
  that *reason,* somehow
    knew how to prostitute itself

April 17, 2000

A SHORT POEM ON THE 20TH CENTURY

never in history
        have so many people
    been killed
in such a short time…
            Again and AGAIN
    the sharpening of
            class struggles
        in their most diverse forms
    while the numbers increased
        of goods produced
                riches accumulated
        people born and saved from
                instant death
    it was also *misery* that increased
                hunger
                despair
            the sense of
        being left alone in a world
            where the rich & mighty
            care mostly for their
                        own good

April 18, 2000

REMEMBERING THE GOOD OLE TIMES

Again, Lindbergh is steering the
shaky little plane
across the Atlantic
Wide and wind-torn expanses
if you know what I mean
Again, people are dying of malaria in the Isthmus
"Here we are," they say,
"digging the *grand* canal!"
Meanwhile, Teddy Roosevelt is rubbing his hands
getting the ship ready
to be exploded
in Habana harbor
In Paris investors are swept off their feet
The Indo-Suez shares thundering
lightning-like
into a black sea below
They had thought it was the Red Sea
but it wasn't / In China
the Boxers, meanwhile, were warming up
How long ago it all seems,
but what are a hundred years in history?
A short stretch of way on the rollercoaster of
human fate
"Human?", you say.
Shrugging, we know you are right.
The *all too inhuman* fate
is man-made.
Right behind your back
you've done it —

joined in
even when asleep
even when unable to see
the white in the tiger's eye
It is always men who are riding the tiger
It is you and me
as it has been
in the case of our forefathers,
and *their* forefathers before them
In a second, history like a film
glides past
and we see
peaceful cities
landscapes devastated by floods
crowds on the run
wars spilling over
the concentration camps of fascism
the post-war boom
with its confounding experiences of amnesia
Again, the tables are turned
the players cornered
the weapons, as concealed as ever
ready to be drawn
Yesterday, Madeleine encountered Putin
What deal was in the offing?
Who was trying to trick whom?
What package were they going to open -
Again, the old box of *Pandora?*

20/2/2000

THE BEAUTY OF LEAVES

1

Looking at a volume of poetry
  I discover the beauty of leaves
they feel good as I touch them
      not too smooth
      not too shiny
    the white subdued
     as if a slight nuance of
     birch tree color had entered the
        paper mass
     taking away some of the
      abstractness of white -
a *white,* like an open sky a field of snow
      a white body
    written on by the paint brush
        of birds
       But it was only
     the pecking finger
     searching for vocals, consonants
      on the keyboard
       of a typewriter
      that had left
                its trace

2

    leafing through a book
      it comes to life

But leaves of books are only
      dead wood
         pulp processed
         into paper

3

when I saw Angelo's woodcut ...
the white, dream-like shape of leaves
              found by chance
        picked up & carried home
     devoid now of their autumn colors
      which will only echo
           in memory -
it was like a mantra
   a Freudian dream carpet picture
 a shrine
      dedicated to
   the life-cycles of all
         leaves, all
            trees

20/2/2000

DOUBLE-CROSSING THEM

It's the old game
    that keeps
        the *hate* alive

that perhaps
    kindles *its flame*
        more than everything

In Chechnya
land of the mountains, plains
land of a suppressed people of
    shepherds, peasants
    forced into exile
        by the bloody one
      driven from the land
      driven into the emptiness
        of the steppes
       of blizzards, hunger
           forced labor -

In Chechnya, again
there is a war going on
  there are towns laid to ashes
    thousands and thousands on the walk
    trying / to stay alive
      trying / to leave the land

villages burning…
      passes mined…

reckless bombing of
herds, way up
in the mountain zones

But who, I ask
encouraged the
invasion of
Dagestan, who
sent money
sent fighters
from Arabia?

Who promised
Shevardnardze
that Georgia would
join NATO?
who is jittery
that the oil
from Baku flow
to Turkey not
Russia?

And still, the listening posts
in far-off Pamir regions
of the trustworthy U.S. ally -
Germany

betray the secrets of
resistance to Russia
They collaborate with the
invaders of Grosny

they, the invaders of old
play their part
in the old, dirty game
double-crossing
the village folk

double-crossing the young men
drunk with the poison of
nationalism
tired by years of
discrimination
to bear the old yoke of
second-class citizenship

They who want justice
who were victims once
in their own way
of German aggression
they pay, today, again
the same bloody prize

May 4, 2000

KARLOVY VARY

the old mansion
　　still owned by the
　　association of
　　　　former sufferers
　　　　　　of NAZI terror

to be "privatized" now
　　It is the wind
　　　　of change
　　the spirit
　　　　of the time

and Pavel
　　whom they sent
　　as an adolescent
　　　　to Theresienstadt
　　the *Kurort*
for those destined to die -
　　　　wantonly advertised
　　　　by the killers
　　　　　　as a nice place, a
　　　　　　　　real resort-town
　　　　for those
　　　　　　they somehow wanted
　　　　　　　　to vanish, from the earth...

"the lazy"
"the rich, and money-hungry"
"the clever-ones"

"too clever to
soil their hands"

is it that / what they thought?
They did not see
you say
the girls toiling in
sweat shops
the watch-maker
the mechanic

They saw them, well enough
and transported them away
into the ovens
into steam and dust
and air and
ashes
for their "Jewishness"
whatever that meant

and the survivors
find no words
find no words
for what was done
or never, the right words
or never -

but wake up
trembling, through the night

The mansion -

the government gave it
in forty-eight
as a token
as a potential support
for the bruised bodies

a crutch
a place to meet
a place of
silent
memories
suppressed

And now they hand it back
to the old owners
who found it came next to nothing
when neighbors
were taken away

May 4, 2000

A CZECH GERMAN GAMBLE

they came, as colonists
into the mountains
welcomed by a king
not the bears

living on the edges
of a kingdom
people imbued with
a faint trace of Roman culture

intrigues, and power-politics
is it that / what charts
the course of political
events, leaves its scars?

kingdoms come and go
people toil, give birth, die
The Hussite wars
Will Viennese injustice top it, ever?

of course, it will
Or *more of that / to come*
And finally, after a big, bloody war
liberation

suppression breeds resentment
a bunch of provincials
priding themselves of first-class citizenship
because of the dialect they speak

suddenly find they are now
in turn, second-class citizens
Victims of suspicion, they think
    They never bothered / to learn Czech

  The Republic
to them, is a foreign land
They long for the Reich
  "Heim," somehow

No Angels, homeward-looking
  but a mixed bunch
  of Social-democrats, Commies, Fascists
But most of them, "Hillbillies"? –
  "A Conservative, Racist Breed?"

  They opened
the Gate of the Castle
  to the Invaders
    Their Blood-Thirsty Brothers

  They killed their own kind
or stood by, motionless
  They marched
  into the next big war

One stupidity, we know
  breeds *another*
and nationalism
    of any kind is a plague

But driven out
of the mountains, the cities
how *few* have learned
the lesson well?

And staying behind
in the mountains, the cities
how *few* have learned
the lesson well?

May 4, 2000

THE STORY, OF OLD

wronged, or feeling wronged, or both
they wronged others, or stood by, looking
the other way when it happened
Is that how it was?
Is that how people are?
And is it, always, again and again
the same old tale
the Wheel of History turning
its bloody Spokes
Or are *we*
turning the spokes
forming the Wheel
making or
breaking it?

May 4, 2000

A FRIEND

The old man
            clutching
the woman who
        took his picture
when he was young

a thin, handsome man
    carrying a bundle of straw
no sandals
        protecting his
        leathery feet

Today, his eyes
        photographed again -
the face, photographed again -
    his hand, his arm
    invisible for us
        embracing the
woman, in her nineties -
    what do they tell?
a long long
        silence -
    what do they tell?
        all those years that passed
    what do they tell?
        she's come back -
        he's still alive
            she is
        she has come back

a friend
falling, how long ago
in another life
a different kharmatic
affair, so to speak
opportunistically
for a career
as a Third Reich filmmaker

how deep, the scar
how long, the turning away
the cleansing
the new life, falling in love with
a barren country
its wronged, impoverished
inhabitants

her dyed hair
her bitter lips
the rouge-wearing face -
how tender, it seems…
how saved
by the love
of an old man

Gabike

Riefenstahl's friend

May 4, 2000

TEIRESIAS

tasting excrements
    raving, ecstatically
in sordid intimacy
    ashen-faced, speechless

a young one
    that went through
            the fire of self-hate

a victim victimized
    fearing to have saved his skin
    always and always and always
        at the expense of some
        third person

    a shadow
    a mother-figure
  a father-figure and
    father's father figure
    the tiny figure of a child

    how did you survive it
    how did you survive -
is that what the *Erinyes* are whisp'ring?
    is this their silent shout
        coming forth from the
            dark gap
            under the ash-tree?
    the channel linking

to the other world –
the *past*
allowing *no* two-way communication

The seer, they have it
has been blinded
by the torturers

May 4, 2000

A LANDSCAPE

The scattered rocks, pieces only
of history / the transmutant
        transforming collection of
marbles stolen, how many years ago,
        from the Acropolis

Again they have been
seduced to leave their place - the British
Museum, but this time
            it is no Lord, it's an artist

who has abducted them
in his somnambulant walk
thru a landscape lighted
            by a distant moon

The moon's light is dangerous
The moon's light has painted
        the landscape red

Lord Elgin's marbles, like haphazard heads
        of buried prisoners
            sprout from the land -

the rolling, rock-strewn land -
    the lava flow of light -
    the scattered rocks -
    the scattered heritage
        of *old* -

No goddess now
No polis
no *Athína*
Merely the grid-pattern of the screen

And the rockets haven't homed in yet
Or have they?

20/2/2000

EREBUS

ere you were
the bus was
traveler Your
destination
forgive
the earth
her lap
waiting

May 4, 2000

AN EVENING, IN THE COUNTRYSIDE

For Micha,
remembering such walks

Approaching the fence
　　suddenly saw the
　　six, or so, calves
　　　　turning towards us
　　throwing up their asses
　　galloping, sort-of
　　　　　　for a few yards

Curiously, they watched
　　　then turned
　　circling downward
　　　towards, it seems
　　　　a water-filled trough

On that walk
　　　into the forest
we passed a raised hide
　　its boarded windows
　　　opened on three sides

and from one, the dark silhouette
　　of a face, half-hidden by the shadow
　　　of a hat's brim
　　　glumly looked at us

fearing our noises, we thought
wishing we'd be far-away
as he lay in ambush
for some deer entering the
peaceful clearing

May 4, 2000

REFLECTIONS ON A STRING SYMPHONY

Written after reading
about a new theory

waves, the wind
the shadow of the hand
moving, across the paper

and wind's waves
stir the leaves
stir the grass
make the little branches *swing* and
dance

and the birds chirp their
little love songs
their songs of warning
of alarm

and all the while
a man sits and thinks
that perhaps
all of this, including the
buzzing flies

is an *illusion*
is a *make-belief*

and the universe is really only
energy

an abstract formula
a symphony of
   myriads of swinging
     one-dimensional strings

May 4, 2000

LOCKERBIE

this startles me:
judges, about to judge
those guilty
of the dead of Lockerbie

villagers
torn from the midst of life
by burning, falling
wreckage of a plane

travelers, at nearly 10 times 10, times
10 kilometers per hour, propelled - through icy air
through strata higher than the Everest
then tumbling, suddenly
between pieces of baggage
packed souvenirs
(another word for: memories)

5 kilometers is the speed - remember?
of persons walking
on a road swept empty
or through the crowd-filled
noise-whipped
greed-driven profit-machines
called towns
that are planned by

investors urbanists
architects

politicians
but never by
the populace inhabiting them

You, too
living in towns that you have not produced
are involved, judges,
in planning the course
of world events
You are to judge
the guilty

But are you
  to find out
all there is to be found
about the chain of events
connecting cause and cause

Where is this flight of thoughts going, where
is it headed - your journey?

And will you, too,
crash?

and where,
and when,
and why?

The press, *Mossad*...
Who spoke of the Syrian trace -
being more factual than the Libyan?

And what is factual in this puzzle?
Who is playing
the Tehran game?

Are you aware, aware of
the cruiser
quietly await,
in the blue Arabian Gulf

the Persian Gulf where they were
contesting –
 not only names...

Are you aware, aware of
the pilgrims
ripped, from their Mecca dream?

Was is true, then
and the commander
of the cruiser
trained in Annapolis couldn't
tell apart
the wide belly of the Iranian jumbo
from a Mig 19 coming from
distant Iraq -

Was this
        what it was like
and therefore
poor Lockerbie, your farmers
mutilated, torn to pieces

the baggage dispersed
over your meadows
the cattle bleeding
tiles broken, under the impact of the fuselage
the coroners of Scotland
Yard with their plastic bags,
oh judges, is this
the whole truth, and why, then
the complaints about the security checks
at Frankfurt Airport where they
let it pass -
uninspected, upon official request:
the deadly suitcase
smuggled they say
for Lebanese drug dealers
by the agents of
some Drug Enforcement Agency

(1999)

I LOVED YOUR PROMISE

America, I loved your promise
your dream of justice, of free and
equal men in pursuit of
human happiness, yes
as a kid
I was *that* naive, today
I read of your best-selling
prescription drugs, against
ulcers -
and high blood pressure, I can
see your young men sitting in their
cars going to work!
Wearing white shirts
they are sweating, in mid-winter!
their faces reddened
their pulse, accelerated by demand after demand
that they make *more* money -
for their company!

America your vaults are flowing
over -
with dollars
while you have emptied the
homeless shelters and asylums, for the insane
spilling their human content
into the streets!

I read statistics that say
there are people earning as little as 5 dollars and a half

six dollars and a half per hour
      in Montana,
Mississippi, Nebraska, Wyoming
The poor get poorer and the rich
richer, but the poor
get also more numerous
in this country of
unlimited possibilities - unlimited
for whom?
for the billionaire who buys politicians?
sends men to Congress
on fat invisible paychecks called fees?

I know they are collected
for so-called advice given
prior to becoming
a candidate

But who
gave whom
what advice?
Who lent his ear,
and who talked?

America, your promises have gone
down the drain
have all been broken except one
that you'll be powerful enough
to blast your deceitful images sky-high
Satellites are orbiting the earth
and tell the poor

of wealth amassed -
ample chances
to strike it rich

Recently they imported
12,000 slaves from Asia -
indentured servants of the
20th century that is drawing to its
ill-famed close

Employers bought these Asian
emigrants thrilled to go
to Miami, to New York City!

They keep them like cattle
They keep them as clandestine property

A dirt-cheap workforce
that netted their importers
an estimated 220 million dollars
in cash

Nov. 25, 1998

THE YOUNG, TODAY

they go
to Daytona,
Panama City
Crazy Beach (Florida)
or to Cancún

they drink
Budweiser Light,
prey
on each other
lookin'
for a good fuck

they have been taught
early, not to
daydream
and they're afraid of
emotions
such as
love

in their nightmares
they always
fear
to be even more alone
than they are

they move with the crowd
opinionwise

their gangs and 'cliques' a shabby
ersatz for the communities
        that never were

but were dreamt of
        nonetheless

Today, the pragmatic ideologues in power
tell them cooperation
        is but a fad of the '60s
        a 'false idea' of some by-gone
        'lunatic fringe'
It is TEAM WORK now
that is, you lose bonuses if
        your "team" is
                        worse
        than the other

'Worse' of course means
less profitable
        for the boss

Instead of a foreman you now
have the team that pays
        for deadlines
        not met on schedule

They called it
        collective guilt
in another age
meaning you're taken hostage

with the others

"Caught together,
hung together"
does that ring a bell?

But they tell you
it's still the best
of all possible worlds
There is no better
system imaginable

Ah, what a poor imagination
you all must have!

April 27, 2000

A RICH MAN'S WORLD

In a rich man's world
    even the poor have everything
  they have sweaters colored
      with chemicals
        that enter the body through your skin
       when sweating
          giving you cancer

  they have towns filled by the exhausts of
     tens of thousands of cars
    they have electro-smog
  and high ozone levels
    PCB's in their groundwater
      and their food

  they have fish no longer safe to eat

their hens and roosters have become
         fish, flapping wings

    eggs smell of fish-meal factories
   they are x-rayed
  so you'll not find a small
     unborn fish inside

 they have corn that is
       genetically manipulated
    and that goes into bread
       as soft as a sponge

their spices have been radiated
		while growing in fall-out covered soil
and again, radiated,
			when harvested -
		this time, "for freshness"

they have cheese packed in plastic
		that soaks up plastic softeners
		and transforms them
			into artificial hormones

they have meat from cows turned into
				meat-eaters
		filled up with antibiotics like the chicks
		fed with growth-
			accelerating substances for
				watery taste and
			some
		develop bovine, spongiform
				encephalous disease

they have nuts bought up cheaply
		by international
				trading corporations
		that have grown moist
				in warehouses
		and that faintly smell
				of mould
			unless salted, or roasted

they even have tomatoes

designed by bio-tech specialists
that still look fresh and
    red as the real thing
           while they rot inside

    they'll win any prize
           for the best strawberry taste
    Or else
one can see them
             spew forth
    their nitrate enriched
                water

Yes, in a rich man's world
    the poor have
        almost everything of this

But, as the saying goes,
    the rich have it too

April 27, 2000

TABLE OF CONTENTS

POSTSCRIPT BY THE EDITOR

Some books don't age, or age slowly. This book of poems was first offered more than two decades ago to a critic and scholar as a book about the Twentieth Century. He disliked it and called it mere "rant."

Now, twenty-two or twenty-three years later, I am surprised very often by the topicality of many poems that Alicia Zukofsky wrote so quickly at the time. They are angry poems in many cases, some are tender, all are pensive, in this or that way. Her erudition is remarkable. Her knowledge of the world amazing. Her emotional intensity confirms Pound's dictum that the quality of a poem depends to a large degree on the strength of the emotion that it makes felt.

Alone, so often, in her small room at the outskirts of the city, Alicia Zukofsky is hesitant when asked about her life experience. She chose to leave the place where she lived and worked for so long, in 2005, opting for exile.

Her memories are bitter but her optimism is unbroken. She says that writers have a task, a burden: To see things clearly, and to warn.

Karen Wittstock